WALKING
WITH THE
SAGE

A Story of Leaving Everything to Find More

WALKING
WITH THE
SAGE

A Story of Leaving Everything to Find More

KATHY ROBINSON

Published by: Collabria Publishing
Athena Wellness Enterprises, LLC, Oakland, NJ

With gratitude and appreciation:
Developmental Editing by: Brooke Adams Law
Copy Editing by: Virginia McCullough
Cover and Book Design by: Asya Blue Design
Author Photo: Sarah Flannery Photography

ISBN 979-8-9941822-0-8 Paperback
ISBN 979-8-9941822-1-5 Ebook

Library of Congress Control Number: 2026901436

BOOKS BY KATHY ROBINSON

*The Athena Principles, Simple Wellness Practices
for Overworked Professionals*

*Walking with the Sage, A Story of Leaving
Everything to Find More*

For the courageous souls navigating the liminal space between who they were and who they are becoming.

PRAISE FOR *WALKING WITH THE SAGE*

In the isolation of the pandemic, Kathy, a newly retired corporate power woman, undertakes daily walks into the woods behind her New Jersey home. Her forays soon invoke a dialogue with inner wisdom, personified as a vibrant 80-year-old future self. Using story to reveal insights that encourage readers to make their own journeys, this is a true-life fable, told in metaphors you will want to underline… and remember… and put into practice for yourself.

—**Christina Baldwin**, author of *The Seven Whispers, Storycatcher, The Beekeeper's Question*, and other titles

As a Wilderness Rites of Passage guide, I can attest to the powerful, life-changing guidance available in nature when we deeply listen. As our guide, Kathy takes us along on her walks in the woods, as she learns to listen in a radical new way and discovers the wisdom within. Her transformative story of midlife change comes more fully alive as the natural world mirrors her wholeness, knowing and truth. Through her curiosity, and vulnerable storytelling, we see that this is possible for each of us, as is trustworthy, ancient wisdom. We need this book in these times.

    —**Sara Harris**, Co-Founder of EarthWays LLC, Board Member and Elder Guide, Veteran Rites

This insightful story invites us to reflect on our own journey and what truly matters. Kathy meets her doubts and fears with grace, compassion and humor – she feels like someone we know, an everywoman navigating the messy middle of transformation. As she learns to trust her inner wisdom, we're reminded that this same wisdom lives within all of us, waiting to be heard when we slow down enough to listen. Her journey lights the way for anyone sensing a quiet whisper that there is something more.

    —**Bobbi Kahler**, Leadership Development Coach & Author of *Travels of the Heart: Developing Your Inner Leader* and the Substack publication *Beautiful Strength*

A NOTE FROM THE AUTHOR

You're about to embark on a journey with Kathy, a successful executive who, like many midlife professionals, finds herself at a crossroads, yearning for purpose beyond corporate success.

While the core themes of her search are drawn from personal and coaching experiences, *Walking with the Sage* is not a memoir. The characters, dialogue and specific sequence of events have been fictionalized, interwoven and shaped to create an engaging narrative.

Consider this book a map that uses storytelling to light the way for the creation of your own vibrant next chapter.

PROLOGUE

Five years earlier

She was striking in presence, a radiant beacon of warmth and wit. Her lean build appeared taller than her 5' frame. Faded jeans that fit just right, comfortable black sweater, and eyes that twinkled behind black framed glasses, prominent against her pure white hair, cut short and casually tousled.

This was the image that stayed with me long after the assignment was completed. I wrote the visualization off as little more than a coaching exercise recommended to help me reimagine my next chapter.

But there was something about the presence of the image I conjured up in my mind as I listened to the meditation. She had something I couldn't name. And I wanted it.

ONE

"Retire!"

That's the word I wrote in the small hardcover notebook I carried to all of my meetings. Then I circled it for emphasis.

Leaning back in my chair, I slunk low, listening to the bank's CEO on the speakerphone, his voice echoing in my closed door office. He briefly outlined the plans for the CFO, my administrative boss, responsible for my day-to-day oversight, to leave the company in the coming year. This was ten days after the announcement that the Audit Committee chairman, my functional boss, responsible for the strategic direction of my work, would relinquish his role the following quarter.

I rubbed my forehead, partly in disbelief and partly to ease the tension rapidly building as I rocked in my desk chair, like it was a leather cradle.

It was 2018. I was only 54 with almost a full year before I'd be eligible to retire. But in that moment, I knew with every fiber of my being that I didn't have the wherewithal to onboard two new bosses. If I had to prove myself to anyone, it would be to me. It was time to leave corporate and start my own business.

The CEO's call lasted all of two minutes, but I was too deflated to move. Instead, I swiveled my chair and stared out the large plate glass windows, letting it all sink in. As the announcement replayed in my head, it was clear that my 30+ year career had changed in an instant.

Taking a deep breath to gather my energy, I stood, my high heels sinking into the plush carpet. I took a moment to steady myself before walking across the office. Then I opened the door and asked my assistant, Mary, to gather my direct reports so I could share the news of our boss's impending departure.

To say this rocked my world is an understatement. After decades of learning the game and climbing the corporate ladder, I had made it to the pinnacle of my profession as a Chief Audit Executive and Chief Risk Officer. I was a trusted advisor to the senior management team and the board. I led a global audit and risk team that performed well and helped the company run optimally. We developed a cutting edge methodology that I shared with peers at professional conferences.

And... there was no doubt it was time to go. But that

didn't stop the gut wrenching fear that reared its head at every turn. At times, the thought of leaving gripped so fiercely that adrenaline spikes caused my stomach to clutch and legs to weaken.

I could almost hear my mother, who'd passed the year before, admonishing me from the beyond. "Are you crazy? You'll never have another opportunity like this. Don't throw away all your hard work!"

My rational self knew this was last century, depression-era programming that I absorbed from my parents. But what if it was true?

During my commutes to and from work, I began to imagine what it would be like to change professions and build my own wellness company. I envisioned flowing workdays, engaging projects and making a difference in the lives of stressed out professionals. While these visualizations felt blissful, I still struggled with the decision.

One morning as I was getting ready for work, the adrenaline began to build until it reached a fevered pitch. I was nauseous as my heart raced and I labored for breath.

In the midst of this panic swirl, a question surfaced. *If you could have only one employee on your new team, who would it be?* The answer came immediately. *Me.*

And with that, this realization. *So why are you fighting this? You've never let yourself down before. Why would you fail in this situation?*

And there it was – an awareness that brought a true sense of calm. My chest expanded and I took an unimpeded deep breath.

This became the antidote. When the fear would rise – and it often did – I would remember that I was betting on myself. And with that thought, it all would ease.

That pattern continued throughout the year.

TWO

Part of me wondered if I had an innate sense that corporate life was coming to an end.

I'd done a lot of searching since turning 50, undercover inner explorations by night as I continued to execute my corporate responsibilities as usual by day, all in an effort to find my way forward.

I attended writing retreats, explored the esoteric in weekend workshops, and spent long hours training outdoors for ultra endurance sports events. I also did a lot of journaling. These varied activities were instinctive ways to shed my external layers and explore the unspoken question: *Who am I when I'm not a corporate professional?*

Rummaging through my old journals, I found notes from a "future self" visualization exercise I had done several years prior. It was based on the idea that when you envision yourself in the future, you tend to make aligned decisions in the present to move in that direction.

I remembered how startling it was to see myself as an 80-year-old. But it wasn't just the physical appearance that captivated me. She exuded vitality, wisdom and a profound sense of peace.

Here's how I captured the visualization in my journal:

As I rounded the corner, I caught a glimpse of the house. It was set high on a hill and ablaze in light, resembling a modern cathedral surrounded by tall pines. After parking at the end of a long line of cars along a sidewalk-less road, I walked uphill towards the front door. Through the trees to my right, I could see the sweeping expanse of a crystal blue body of water.

I rang the doorbell and took a step back. A rush of apprehension took me by surprise followed by a tinge of nervous nausea. I took a deep breath and felt it lessen. As I waited, I could hear laughter, conversation and background music – the sounds of celebration.

When the door opened, I extended my hand to the greeter and introduced myself, which instantly felt a little too formal. She smiled and stepped forward to give me a welcoming hug, saying, "Hello, sweetheart, welcome." I was immediately at ease.

She took my hand gently but firmly, and we began to move through the mingling guests with a swift grace that belied her 80 years. She held a small tumbler of bourbon on the rocks in her other hand that she never seemed to sip, a subtle accessory to her infectious presence.

As we glided around the glass-enclosed home, she stopped periodically to introduce me to a number of guests, offering food and drink, and talking about the home, which she bought when she retired. Her voice was rich with the cadence of a seasoned storyteller.

I spent the afternoon and evening socializing with the guests, an eclectic mix of folks from all walks of life that seemed to somehow fit together at this gathering. I felt included, understood the humor and was engaged in conversation.

Even as the party buzzed with excitement, I could feel a sense of quiet satisfaction, a deep pride in the life she had built and the stories she had woven.

At one point, the crowd gathered and a toast was made – to a <u>New York Times</u> bestseller and the *joy of being a writer in this beautiful community. And then another, for celebrating 20 years of partnership. "I'm still in love with life, work and my beloved," the author said as she raised her glass and turned to kiss her partner.*

As the evening wound down, I gathered my things and she walked me to the door. We stood on her porch, the cool breeze ruffling her hair. She stared at the horizon where the sky met the shore. I could feel a sense of peace settling over her, a contentment born of a life well-lived.

She turned to me and smiled. "Be well, sweetheart." We put our arms around each other for a parting hug.

I closed the journal, steeped in the feeling of living a life like hers, so different from my current one. And I understood, without question, that this is what my upcoming journey was all about.

THREE

t soon became a habit. Whenever my chest would tighten and my stomach clutch, or I'd imagine myself walking into an irrevocable abyss, I reminded myself that yes, retiring was a risk, but I'd find a way.

I casually floated the idea to family and friends to gauge reaction. "Coming up to 55 next year. I'll be eligible for early retirement, anytime I want." The responses were always some version of "That's great, good for you!" They were genuinely happy for my situation, but since it didn't seem imminent, the topic would shift to something else.

There was relief when the conversation changed because I knew it defied logic. Why leave a good paying job with nothing tangible on the horizon but a dream? Yet, despite my fears, I knew this was the right thing for me to do.

The only way to deal with the fear was to connect with the sense of calm I felt when I got quiet. I would stop what I was doing, close my eyes, and move into the knowingness that I was making the appropriate choice for myself.

I relied more and more on this practice as I readied myself to make it official. It was my ability to call in the feeling of peace that gave me the confidence to first tell my boss, then the CEO, then the board of directors, that I was leaving.

Before each conversation, I prepared myself to stand firm in my decision when the inevitable onslaught of "Why? Are you sure?" questions came my way.

Once this small circle of senior executives became aware of my plans, I was asked to not make an announcement until the new CFO was hired, which was months away. This put me in a strange limbo of keeping my future plans quiet while leading the team. Holding this news felt like keeping a secret, a queasy feeling that became part of my everyday existence for four and a half months.

Whenever I got bogged down in the everyday, I wondered what my 80-year-old author self would think of this drama. I'd think of her kind, joyful, rooted presence, the opposite of what I was feeling in the moment, and know that somehow I was moving toward that place.

I imagined myself sitting in Adirondack chairs with my beloved at sunset, sharing a glass and a rundown of the day. Those brief glimpses were filled with love, depth and stillness. As glorious as that looked, the skeptic, pragmatic audit executive in me wondered if it was actually possible, or worse, if those imaginings were nothing more than a siren's call.

What I did know was that I was tired of living by default. I was intent to design a future that looked and felt "like me," whoever she was these days.

FOUR

Time seemed to both slow down and speed up during my last year of corporate life. The days dripped by, as I summoned my strength to put my game face on and do what was needed, so I could leave in a manner that made me proud. Conversely, the months seemed to speed by, like a countdown clock of paychecks that would soon end.

I embarked on a world tour of sorts, visiting team members and key stakeholders across the globe one last time. Ensuring all loose ends were tied up was important to me. I knew my successor would have their own way of handling things, but for continuity, I felt it was critical for them to inherit a clean slate.

But I was still in an odd state of limbo since the announcement wasn't official. At each stop, my colleagues were unaware this would be my final visit. I was grateful for the opportunity to spend some quality time and thank them for their collegial partnership.

And the whirlwind of airports, hotels and town hall meetings kept my mind occupied.

In rare quiet moments, I wondered what my new life would feel like. I imagined a more leisurely existence, filled with intrigue, exploration and new experiences. My new life felt spacious, like it had a flow of its own.

But that vision was far from my current reality. To bridge the gap, I hired a business coach for some entrepreneurial guidance. In my spare time and on the many flights I took that last year, I studied for a wellness coaching certification and worked on the business infrastructure to support my practice.

I also decided that in order to be successful right out of the gate, it was critical to have my wellness philosophy documented. My plan was to codify all the techniques I used throughout the years to keep myself well so other professionals had a simple framework to do the same.

I set a goal to complete a book draft by the time I left the corporate world. During a long flight home from India, I created an outline of the principles I would research and the stories I would incorporate, along with a writing schedule. To achieve this, I planned to set the coffee pot for 3:45am each weekday to get an hour of writing in before my workout and workday.

It worked. The book draft was completed during the last week of my corporate career.

It felt odd walking into the building on my final day, November 1, 2019. It was a routine I'd been through each workday for 15 years at that firm. But this time, I'd be turning in my computer and phone before a final meeting with the CEO to thank him for his support over the years.

I left feeling confident that I had done all I could to prepare well for this transition. What I didn't realize as I walked out the door for the last time was that I was also leaving behind more than three decades worth of my identity.

FIVE

I was clicking on all cylinders the first four months of "retirement." Working with a proofreader and designer to ready my first book for publication in May was a new experience. I was also finalizing the design of a new conversion van I planned to use to promote the book across the country. I even met a new love interest.

On New Year's Eve day, I wrote a brief journal entry welcoming 2020, declaring it to be "The best year ever!"

It all came to a screeching halt in early March. I was at a writer's retreat in Washington state when we began to hear that a virus, first reported in January, was spreading. The first case in the United States had been reported in the county next to where I was staying.

Ten writers were working and staying in a large farmhouse, sharing communal space and meals. By the end of the week, we were mindful of our proximity and hygiene, while still blissfully unaware of what was to come.

It became evident, however, as I walked through an eerily empty Sea-Tac airport to head back to New Jersey, that the situation was more dire than we could have imagined.

Even so, the east coast was still largely unaffected. The week of my return, I attended a concert at Madison Square Garden with a group of friends and 20,000 other concert fans. Later that week, I was back in a New York City recording studio for a two day session to lay down tracks for my audiobook.

By the weekend, however, New Jersey announced an impending lockdown. I also decided to end my three month relationship. On St. Patrick's Day, I sat alone in my kitchen as the world seemed to implode. This was not the future I had envisioned.

I reread my New Year's Eve journal entry about 2020 being the best year ever. *Grow the relationship, start the business, finish the book, take the van on a cross-country book tour, enjoy this new life!*

The reality? Isolation.

SIX

t felt like being shuttled onto a giant roller coaster and hurtling into the dark. Where was this all going? One place not to look was the news, which kept a body count ticker in the lower right hand corner of the television screen 24/7.

My primary concern was my 98-year-old father, who was locked down in a retirement home – no visitors allowed. Nursing facilities were hit hard in the New York City area, and although his entire family was close by, we could do nothing for him.

Information from the facility was scarce. Thanks to daily video chats, we were able to see from a distance how he was faring.

My dad was nonplussed by it all. Even at his advanced age, he was able-bodied and had full mental capacity, so he was able to care for and entertain himself. As an introvert, he didn't mind staying in his room and having his meals delivered. He passed the time by reading, listening to music and watching YouTube videos of the big bands he saw in the 1930s and 40s.

My secondary concern was my business. While I dutifully followed the publishing plan I developed when I finished the book draft, I had no idea how to run an online venture. It wasn't long before the old fears began to surface again, especially as the paychecks began to wane.

SEVEN

The Amazon box arrived with an unceremonious thud at my front door. I never got into the package scrubbing routine, but I did leave the carton near the door and went to get a box cutter. Careful not to damage the contents, I opened the box and caught my breath. In my hands was an author's copy of the wellness book I'd spent almost two years writing.

I stood there, staring at the book, delighted with the artwork and the beautiful layout. The matte cover felt so good as I fanned the pages over and over.

I didn't know what to do with this surge of energy and elation. I paced the foyer, throwing my head back with raised arms and shouting, "Yes! I did it!"

But the brief euphoria gave way to the realization that any plans I had to share this lifelong dream with others in person would not come to fruition. I'd need to find other ways to promote and distribute my book. My future plans were reliant on its success.

Visiting my father was a challenge. Exchanging masked waves behind plates of glass, him on the inside of the facility, me on the outside, made no sense to him. He preferred to video chat in the privacy of his room. But I persuaded him to take the elevator down to the lobby so an inscribed copy of my book could be handed to him by a caregiver, after being swabbed, of course.

I was standing in the outside courtyard, watching him take the envelope and walk down the hallway to where we could stand face to face. He took the book out of the package and gave it a long look. When he held it up, I snapped a selfie with him in the background, trying to maneuver my phone to minimize the reflection off the glass. His expression, which I hoped was a smile, was masked. Literally.

Even though we never got to hug, I enjoyed the brief encounter, and was reassured by witnessing his energy level that he was doing just fine in lockdown.

But within weeks of that visit, I received the call we were all dreading. He was isolated in the hospital wing of the facility after testing positive for COVID.

EIGHT

The first week of my father's quarantine was distressing. We were unable to visit him and the staff was so fraught and overwhelmed by the influx of patients that it was hard to get a straight answer from the doctor.

The time between updates seemed like eternity. The television news was filled with stories of fractured families unable to support their loved ones who were suffering through their last days. My siblings and I agreed that if it was his time, we were at peace with his passing. He had lived a long life. Our prayer was: *Please don't let him suffer.*

What was most curious, though, is that my 98-year-old father never exhibited a symptom. Not a cough nor a fever nor any respiratory distress. And this agitated him.

"I don't have COVID!" he would rant into his tablet camera. "I want to go back to my room!"

"Dad, they tested you repeatedly. They even sent the specimens to different labs. They all came back positive. You'll put others at risk if you return to your room. And when you do test negative, there will still be a required quarantine period. You just have to wait it out."

"Jesus Christ," he would mumble in disgust.

"Dad, do you know how lucky you are? People are dying from this in ways you can't imagine."

"I just want to go back to my room."

And so it would go each day for almost a month. He'd complain they were keeping him quarantined for no reason, and his three kids, who would call him each day, would be relieved that this elderly man was somehow beating the odds that were stacked against him.

When the staff finally cleared him to return to his room, he received a hero's welcome as he walked down the hallway, all the residents poking their masked faces out of their rooms and applauding the man who achieved the impossible. He was their superhero. And ours, too. It would be another year before we'd be able to put our arms around him and give him a hug.

NINE

With the family crisis behind me, it was time to get creative on how to promote a new book during a global pandemic. My plans of loading up the van and doing a cross-country book tour were scrapped. So I turned to podcasts, hiring a promoter to book me on a dozen shows.

I'll never forget the first one, a podcast for CEOs who were interested in keeping themselves well. I was stunned when the host introduced me as a "wellness expert" and had a transcendent moment where time seemed to halt altogether.

That's me?! I thought. Then I exchanged some pleasantries with the host and the conversation began. My new life as an author was officially launched.

By mid-June, my days were filled with preparation for the interviews and long nights of learning how to run my own business. The pace felt relentless and my Type-A tendencies kicked in with a vengeance. I could feel my cortisol levels increase, along with a strong undercurrent of fear that I might not be cut out to be an entrepreneur.

So I did what I had done best throughout my corporate career. I blocked out anything extraneous, set my gaze on the next task and plowed through, then jumped on the next one. It was my way of quieting my mind, of not letting myself entertain the thought, *What if this doesn't work out?*

My Plan B had always been going back to corporate life. But as the months elapsed, I was getting the sense that the world had changed so much in such a short time, that I couldn't go back, even if I wanted.

I dug in. Before each interview, I would listen to several of the host's podcast episodes, prepare copious notes and rehearse as if I were giving a board presentation. In addition, there were always business infrastructure updates, blogs to write and attempts at business development.

Those were the good days. But the simplest things could derail it, like when the WIFI went down or the printer stopped working. In my previous life, I would just call out, "Ma-ry!," and help would be on the way. Now, there was no one to call.

The long days bled into marathon evenings. And some nights, I stumbled the 20 feet from my home office to my bedroom at two in the morning, only to rise a few hours later to do it all again.

Had I traded my well-worn corporate treadmill for a new model? With no time to entertain that thought, I pushed it away to focus on the next task on what was becoming a never-ending to-do list.

As the weather warmed, the state and county parks began to slowly reopen. This brought throngs of people out of their hermetically sealed homes and into nature. State police were assigned to the parking areas, closing off the traffic flow once they were filled.

I was lucky. My house was steps away from a little known unmarked path that led to hiking trails. It was so far off the beaten path that few people found their way to my corner of thousands of acres of reserve land.

Each day, for the sake of my mental health, I would make myself close the laptop, put on hiking boots and slip into the mountains to fill my lungs with fresh air and feel the tree-refracted sunshine on my skin.

It was there that I could let all that was bubbling inside come to the surface. It was there I could wrestle with all that was unsettled. And it was there that I could experience the magical transformation of nature's alchemy.

Inevitably, I would return to my waiting laptop for the next business task, refocused and ready to try again.

TEN

As the summer began and the strangeness of 2020 continued, my walking reflections started to deepen.

It was clear that life as we once knew it, and as I had lived throughout my adult life, was not returning. I had made a pivotal decision to leave the safety of my corporate career and go out on my own. At the same time, every aspect of life in the external world had shifted.

What does my future hold in this strange new world?

This is the question I was holding as I walked the now-familiar secluded path into the quiet of the woods. And I was desperate for answers.

Yet, I couldn't focus and felt unusually agitated. There was a churning in my midsection. My head felt buzzy, my steps unsteady. What the hell was going on?

My walks had been my solace – like being dipped in a vat of endorphins. I always came home feeling calm. But the further I walked that day, the more unsettled and confused I became.

"What am I going to do?" I shouted out loud.

"You don't *have* to do anything," came a response.

I was startled and spun around to see an empty trail. *Did I hear that? Did I think that?*

"Who are you?" I asked. Followed inexplicably by, "What are you?"

"Sweetheart, you asked what you needed to do. I'm simply suggesting that you consider doing nothing at all."

"*What the...?*" Did whomever I was in dialogue with know what just flashed through my mind? "It's happened. Weeks in isolation, the pressures of a new business, an upside-down world – I'm finally losing it."

"Sweetheart," I heard again, "take a deep breath. Gather yourself. This is so unlike you."

"Unlike me? How do you know?" I asked. "What is going on?"

I was about to ask who I was telepathically communicating with when something familiar struck a chord. It was the word *sweetheart*. Where had I heard that before?

I walked in silence for a while, thankful not to be in conversation with an unnamed entity. And it hit me. That visualization exercise all those years ago, the *me* from the future. When we met she said, "Hello, sweetheart." And as we stood outside her home saying goodbye, she said, "Be well, sweetheart."

Not sure how to phrase my question, I asked, "Are you me?"

The answer came immediately, "Well, love, I'm a part of you."

"But how? Why? How does this work? Am I talking to myself?"

I could almost hear her chuckle. "The mechanics aren't important. What is of the utmost importance is that you can hear me. And I'm so delighted to be in conversation with you. Although, you're not looking too excited to be chatting with me."

"No, um, I, I am. I'm just so confused. I feel a little queasy, actually."

"How about taking a few breaths?"

I did what she suggested. And yes, it helped. "Maybe the virus finally caught up with me. Maybe this is delirium."

"Do you really believe that's the case?"

"I just don't know how to explain a conversation that feels real but isn't."

"My, my, you have deep grooves."

"What?!" This stopped me in my tracks. The judgment.

"Mmm, and sensitive, too. Well, sweetheart, if it weren't for the sensitivity, we wouldn't be having this conversation, now would we?"

"You can read my thoughts," I said as it dawned on me how invasive that felt.

"I am you, love, remember? I just have a different perspective, one that you called in, I might add. I'm not here uninvited."

"I invited you? How?"

"Sweetheart, there'll be plenty of time for questions. The world is in a bit of a lockdown pattern, if you haven't noticed."

At least she has a sense of humor, I thought and realized she picked up on that, too.

"I think we should call it a day. You look exhausted, love."

"Hard to argue," I said, turning around to head home. "What happens next?"

"Well, that's up to you, sweetheart. I'm here to talk about anything that might be helpful during this time in your life. I suggest you get some rest, think about your most pressing question, and meet me back here tomorrow."

And with those instructions, I felt her recede, as if the line was disconnected.

When I got home, I walked to the cabinet to retrieve a bottle of bourbon that had remained untouched throughout the pandemic, adding a healthy pour into a snifter. The liquor burned as it went down. I took a deep breath and felt the warmth rise and my body relax. It would take another glass before my mind did the same.

ELEVEN

woke up feeling tired from a restless night. My body was still processing the alcohol and I was reminded why I rarely drank anymore. I used to metabolize it better and would wake feeling fine. Now it disrupted my sleep.

My thoughts immediately flashed to my walk and I began to discern whether it was a dream or it actually happened. I experienced something, but I was unsure what had transpired.

I got up, took a run on the treadmill in my basement, showered, and was at my computer, coffee in hand, ready to get to work by eight.

After working through the morning and having lunch, I headed out for my walk, curious if I'd be walking alone or with company.

I was less than a quarter mile up the mountain trail when I heard, "Back for more? I'm so glad you returned, sweetheart."

Well, I guess it wasn't a fluke.

"So, do you have a question for me?"

I walked for a bit, unsure how to articulate the knot that took up residence in my stomach. "I, I don't know how things work anymore," I stammered, so softly I barely heard myself. Apparently, this wasn't an issue for her.

"Yes, I can see that, sweetheart. Tell me more."

"I don't know, it's like everything I learned in school and at work, it's like nothing is applicable anymore. Like all the things I was taught mattered – don't."

We walked in silence as I gathered my thoughts. "As a young adult entering the professional world, life seemed like a puzzle that I needed to figure out, like how to navigate partnership, family and work.

"Throughout my career, there were mentors I turned to for guidance, those who were willing to show me the way and invest their time, energy and belief in me. Whenever someone I truly admired crossed my path, I studied their approach and emulated that behavior.

"Over time, not only did I solve the work puzzle, I got good at the game. When I finally reached the apex of my profession, I chose to leave it, to go out while I was on top, on my own terms. And I had big plans. I put a stake in the ground and claimed this second chapter would be even more successful than my corporate career.

"I'm doing all I set out to do. But now, it's like I don't even know what game I'm playing anymore. Nothing makes sense. I don't get it."

"Oh sweetheart," she said, "you're just in the goo!"

"The what?"

"The goo."

"Explanation, please."

"You're walking the path from your head to your heart. It happens when you stop living like you believe you should and begin aligning with what's true for you today. It's a process of letting go of outdated expectations. This inner journey needs quiet and space to unfold, which is where you find yourself now."

"Okay. But what does that have to do with goo?"

"You left your corporate life prepared to create a new one. From an external perspective, you had everything you needed. You worked with a coach, drafted your book, got certified as a coach yourself, and created your business, all while wrapping up your corporate responsibilities.

"But what you didn't anticipate when you walked through the doors of your former employer for the last time, was the inner metamorphosis taking place."

"Inner metamorphosis?" The concept had never occurred to me.

"It's like when a caterpillar becomes a butterfly. When you experience a catalytic event, a natural reaction is to wrap yourself in a cocoon, to surround yourself with some level of comfort and protection. Since you left corporate life, your safety, your cocoon, has been your plan. You created a six month plan to publish your book and that kept your logical brain pacified by staying focused and busy. But your metamorphosis was happening simultaneously without you even knowing it."

"That makes sense, but what does that have to do with goo?"

"Here's how the process works in nature. When it's time for a caterpillar to transform, it hangs upside down from a branch and spins itself a cocoon. The caterpillar releases an enzyme that melts it into liquid – the goo – which activates special cells that reassemble it into a new form, a butterfly.

"You're in the goo, the messy, yet necessary, early stages of metamorphosis. Your old identity is dissolving and there's an emotional grieving process in letting go of who you were. While there's a natural intelligence to this process, it's not neat and linear, the way you like it."

"Emotional grieving?" I briefly reflected before continuing, "It's been such a jumble of non-stop emergencies from what's happening in the world to keeping tabs on my father and getting a new business up and running. So I understand what you're saying, but I'm still not sure what to do."

"That's just it, sweetheart, there's nothing to do but let the process unfold. Think of the butterfly. It knows how to construct itself as it transforms. It becomes who it's meant to be. That's what's happening for you. But it is a process.

"Even when the butterfly is fully formed, it's still too weak to break out of the cocoon. In fact, it's the struggle to break free that builds the strength for its new life. Once outside, its wings expand and it becomes capable of flight. But that only happens when it lets go of the old caterpillar baggage that's no longer useful. Only then can it trust the unknowingness that lies ahead."

"Unknowingness, I get that."

"It may not feel like it, but this time has been medicine for you. You're in a cocoon, safely held as you reassemble, gather strength, and, in time, expand your wings to take flight. But don't underestimate the power of this quiet time as you transform.

"In fact, the deeper you can connect with your inner self, your still point, the easier this process will become. Your still point is a space of calm. It's where you can detach from your thoughts and emotions in a peaceful place of surrender and release, as natural as a wave rising, falling and returning to the ocean.

"Don't you find it fascinating that you intuitively knew you needed daily walks in nature? That's connecting with your still point."

"I don't feel very still," I said, dismissing the compliment. "I feel mixed up and agitated."

"Well, love, it takes practice, like anything else you've mastered in your life. You need to practice leaving the noise and intensity of modern life and relaxing into the peace and ease that's always available. These mindful pauses will help you take good care of yourself and make the best choices in the present moment. I can teach you a simple practice you can try, if you'd like."

"Sure, I'll try."

"When you wake up tomorrow morning, set your timer for five minutes. Put your right hand over your heart, take a few deep breaths and say to yourself, 'For the next five minutes, there is nothing for me to do and no decision to make.' Just be and enjoy that present moment and see how that feels."

"That's it? Just breathe for five minutes, that's all?"

"That's all."

It didn't seem like much of a game plan, but I agreed to give it a try. I sighed as I turned to head home. "See you tomorrow?"

"I'll be here, sweetheart, rest well."

TWELVE

When I woke the next morning, I set my timer for five minutes, put my hand over my heart and began to deepen my breath. I silently repeated the instructions to focus myself: *There are no decisions to make and nothing to do. Just breathe.*

Almost immediately, my mind drifted to the day's to-do list. I caught myself and refocused. *There's nothing to do, there are no decisions to make in this moment.* More breathing and then another drift to the day ahead. The next thing I knew the alert was sounding.

I turned it off and sat up. It wasn't the transcendental experience I had imagined. It was frustrating, but at the same time I felt relaxed. *Must be the breathing.*

The plan for the day was to follow-up with a potential coaching client, explore new avenues for additional business opportunities, and prepare for upcoming podcasts. But when I opened my laptop to get to work, the first thing I did was type "metamorphosis" into the search bar. I needed something tangible.

I quickly learned the word's very essence was "transformation." Then I dug into the science.

The biological explanations on my screen reminded me of life's intricate orchestration. Hormones precisely governed the process: one drove the caterpillar's growth, while another actively prevented metamorphosis. The profound transformation was triggered only when this second hormone strategically declined, allowing the first to surge and initiate the next phase.

But it was the mention of something called imaginal discs that fascinated me. Buried in the caterpillar were dormant cell clusters, not yet wings or antennae, but their blueprint. The caterpillar's future was already embedded within it.

Then came the chrysalis, where the caterpillar's body underwent histolysis – a complete cellular breakdown. It was programmed cell death, crucial for removing unnecessary larval structures.

This was the goo. The caterpillar didn't resist dissolution – it surrendered to its inherent biological wisdom.

I closed my laptop. It was time for a walk.

THIRTEEN

As I climbed the path, I noticed I felt calmer than on other days and wondered if it had something to do with how my morning began.

"Of course it does, sweetheart, that's why I offered the suggestion."

That was fast, I didn't even summon her.

"You actually did, thinking about our last conversation. I'm so glad you gave it a try. If you choose to continue, you'll see more and more benefit of having time that's completely yours. It'll pay dividends. You'll naturally want to spend more time there."

I wasn't sure what she meant by *there*, but she continued and answered my question before I could ask.

"Isn't it amazing that simply knowing you have a choice to pause and make a little space in your life can relax your mind and bring some peace? All because you're mindfully choosing to just be and enjoy the quiet of the present moment."

I let that sink in. There was some truth in it for me, but I wondered if it could lead to all the benefits she just meticulously outlined.

We walked in silence, which I enjoyed. I breathed in the mountain air, listened to the stream run on my right as I climbed the path, and noted the cardinals, bluejays and pileated woodpeckers as they flew by. It was good to be submerged in nature.

"Why does today feel different?" I asked.

"You're dancing on the edge of heart-based living. You're getting a taste of the oneness of all things."

"Oneness? What does that mean?"

"It's what you're feeling right now, a sense of interconnectedness with your surroundings. It can be difficult to feel any sense of unity between yourself and the Universe when you're busy scaling the corporate ladder."

I found myself nodding in agreement, flashing back to global travel and time zone changes. I remembered a typical trip where I flew to Australia for a two-day meeting, spending less than 72 hours there before a ten-hour flight to Shanghai for another few days of meetings. That pattern continued for decades in India, South America, Northern Africa, Europe and throughout the U.S., a blur of airports, hotels and office buildings, with little time for feeling connected to my surroundings.

"With practice, you may even learn to deepen your sense of oneness and trust it."

"Why would I want to do that?"

"Because when you're deeply aware of the interconnectedness of all things, you become more self-reliant."

"I've always prided myself on being self-reliant," I said, a little too quickly and with a noticeable edge.

"You've been independent, making decisions about the direction of your life, but this is deeper. With practice, you can develop a greater ability to draw from your own reserves of inner wisdom and strength instead of unreliable external sources."

Something felt right about what she was saying but I had no point of reference to form a response.

Then she said, "Quite simply, you've been a warrior, but you yearn to be a sage."

"A warrior?" I said as if it were the most preposterous thing I ever heard. Then I repeated it, "A warrior? I get the independence thing, but a warrior?"

"Oh sweetheart, you exuuude warrior qualities," she said, drawing out the word *exude* for effect. "The drive, focus and discipline. You've set goal after goal and when you achieve one, you never even stop to pause, you just head straight for the next one."

"That's true."

"And you love a good competitive challenge. Your direct, action-oriented approach made you a successful leader who got results. And it's that relentless treadmill of achievement that got you here today."

"Okay, I see that."

"You've been on quite a hero's journey, shaped by a continuous cycle of heeding the call of the next goal, overcoming any challenges and obstacles that got in the way, and successfully completing the task.

"But that was the past. You spun your cocoon because you desire something more. You stepped off the treadmill, while it was going full speed, I might add. You descended the ladder you spent decades dutifully climbing. You *chose* to leave. Why?"

"It was complete." I spoke so quickly I surprised myself. I gave it a little more thought and added, "It felt like there was nothing more to do or to prove. I would just be repeating myself and keeping the status quo, which wasn't interesting to me."

"Did you ever think that maybe it wasn't the work that felt complete, but the way you lived your life?"

I didn't see that coming. It stopped me in my tracks. *How I lived my life? Was that why it was so clear it was time to go?*

"Tell me more," was all I could think to say.

FOURTEEN

"Let's talk about your caterpillar self, we'll call her Corporate Kathy. Tell me about her."

"Well," I said, pausing to gather my thoughts. "You did a pretty good job of describing her. She was self-motivated, results-oriented and disciplined. Direct. Corporate Kathy was a straight-shooter who kept things on track and played by the rules."

"Yes, yes, but how did she *feel*?"

"How did she feel? She wasn't paid to feel."

"Ooh, very old school," she said. *Was that a mock?* "How did she feel when she wasn't at the office?"

"I don't know, like a normal person, I guess. Partner, family, friends, you know, the usual feelings of love and connection."

"So her life was bifurcated then. She was one person at work and another at home?"

"Yeah, I think that's fair. She didn't bring much of her personal life into the office."

"So she really couldn't be authentic then, could she?"

I groaned at the word *authentic*, like an audible eye roll. "Look, you know what she did for a living. It was her job to make sure that the firm was conducting its business efficiently, effectively and ethically. The overwhelming majority of employees were, but in the cases where someone wasn't playing by the rules, there were consequences. It would have been *inauthentic* if she came across as everyone's best friend and then brought the gauntlet down when it was needed. It was better to keep a distance."

"And now? Does the Corporate Kathy warrior persona still live on?"

I got quiet. "I don't know. I left that world and then we all wound up in lockdown."

After giving it some thought, I said, "I guess something shifted because it's a weekday morning and I'm walking in the mountains talking to you." I paused, "That last part came out jerkier than I meant it to."

"No worries, sweetheart. There's never any judgement here. But you did hit on an important truth. Things have shifted. That's exactly what has brought you to the mountains, and to me."

"Please continue," I said, feeling like we were on the edge of an important insight.

"A few minutes ago when you described Corporate Kathy, how did that make you feel?"

"Hmm, a mix of things. Exhausted by how 'on' she had to be all the time."

Digging deeper, I added, "Empathetic that she did it for so many years. Proud that she earned everything that came her way."

But there was something else I couldn't quite articulate. After walking a little further, I admitted, "And a little sad that the game is over, but relief that I don't have to play anymore. Does any of this make sense?"

"Perfect sense."

We walked in silence before she said, "Let me ask you this: Who is the opposite of Corporate Kathy, your butterfly self?"

I let out a long exhale, like the question packed a punch. "I don't know."

"Sure you do, sweetheart. Let's try it another way. Name a quality she might have."

"Well, I guess she'd be the opposite of bifurcated. Whole?"

"Lovely – we'll call her Wholly Kathy."

I chuckled at the pun and clarified, "That's W-H-O-L-L-Y, not H-O-L-Y?"

She chuckled back. "Yes, W-H."

"It's hard for me to find the words. To use your phrases, less warrior-like and more sage-like?" I was grasping at straws.

"How about this, sweetheart. Tomorrow when you wake and do your five minute breathing practice, think about the words *Wholly Kathy*. Meet me back here tomorrow and tell me all about her."

FIFTEEN

The next morning when I woke, I set my timer for 10 minutes instead of five to allow for the drifting I experienced the day before. I settled back in bed, put my hand over my heart, took a few deep breaths, and brought the words *Wholly Kathy* to mind.

My mind's eye was a blank slate, but I experienced a profound feeling of calm, like taking a warm bath. I felt peaceful. So much so that I must have drifted back to sleep and jumped when the timer went off 10 minutes later. Even so, the deep peace still permeated my body.

It stayed with me throughout the day, like I was riding a surfboard instead of swimming against the current, the way I felt most mornings. I sent off the proposal to the potential coaching client. There was even a new business opportunity that looked promising.

The day was going so smoothly that I found myself at a stopping point around lunchtime. I ate a salad before putting on my boots and heading out for my afternoon hike. I was halfway up the mountain path before I heard, "You're glowing today."

That made me laugh out loud. "Glowing?"

"I'm getting the sense that you got some insight this morning."

"Well, I did feel an incredible sense of calm, but then I fell asleep. Not sure I would say I got enlightened."

"Tell me about the calm."

"It started at the top of my head and then slowly entered my body, very slowly, like the way honey pours."

"How did it make you feel?"

"Like I was rooted. It was peaceful and quiet. The exact opposite of Corporate Kathy."

"Mmm, indeed."

I could feel a question brewing and tried to gather the words. "So, how does this work? Corporate Kathy is stressed but gets things done, while Wholly Kathy is calm but gets lulled to sleep? How does this approach help me build a successful business?"

"It's true you can't sleep through the business building process, but do you need to continuously stress about it? Think back to why you started taking these walks."

I scanned my recent memory. "At first, it was just to get out of the house since we were unable to go anywhere else. It was a way to enjoy the spring, which turned into summer."

"What about the day when we first, shall we say, met?"

"Yeah, I was spinning my wheels."

"And why was that?"

"Things weren't happening as quickly as I thought they would."

"Yes, you were trying to make things happen."

"That's right, it always worked before. But now, it feels like the harder I push, the less I get done. I get so frustrated."

"But this morning felt different?"

"Yeah, this morning felt like I was in flow."

"Exactly! And you didn't need to push?"

"No, the day unfolded."

"Yes, that's the difference between the approaches of a warrior and a sage, making something happen versus allowing it to happen."

I walked in silence and reflected on how I'd started the day. Then I began to recount what I experienced. "I tried to connect with the words *Wholly Kathy*, fell back to sleep, woke with a start and yet, I carried that feeling of...what's the word I'm looking for...*presence*?"

"That's right, love," she said. "You were present today. That's the entry point for everything you yearn for, which is being in the moment. And it's as simple as calling it in, just like you did this morning."

"It feels so passive. I'm used to making things happen."

"The warrior and the sage are not mutually exclusive. In fact, when you're in true balance, they each play an important part. You've always had qualities of both. Your mighty warrior just took the lead – always." There was that chuckle again.

"So now I want my sage to take the lead?"

"You tell me, sweetheart. It seems that's why you're here, talking to me on this mountain path.

"It's not as complex as you think. Your sage self can get things done, but she comes from a place of wisdom, compassion and service. She approaches life contemplatively and is motivated by inspiration."

"Sounds like a tall order."

"It's the natural state of the butterfly self. It just takes a bit of time. I can share some practices, if you'd like. It will give your warrior self something to focus on."

"What do you mean by practices? Why should I practice?"

"The first step in engaging with your sage self is creating a quiet space to connect at your deepest level. That's actually what happened to you this morning. You know you're there when you get that calm, peaceful feeling. Practices are a way to invite that space to open up."

I let her words seep in as I enjoyed the walk and the day.

SIXTEEN

walked to a favorite spot and sat down, my back resting against the trunk of an old oak tree. "I'd like to hear more. Which practice is the best?"

"The one you love to do and do often. And the only way to find it is to practice."

"To practice practicing?"

"Exactly."

"Very meta. Okay, what do you suggest?"

"You're looking for something that will help you develop new levels of self-awareness. The more intentional you are when you perform the activity, the more the practice will support your life choices. I suggest you start with small steps, like you did with your breathing practice. All practices can be scaled over time if you want to go deeper with them."

"Makes sense. What are my options?"

"Practices you may find most helpful include contemplation, journaling, positive action and holding a question. As you'll see, you can even mix and match them. But first, let me tell you about each.

"Contemplation simply means reflective thought, which is the state of mind and spirit Wholly Kathy is looking to nurture. You can get to this state in a number of ways, including meditating, visualizing or what you're already doing, intentional walks in nature and your morning breathing practice. Get creative. You can gaze at the ocean or night sky, if you like. Anything that invites presence will work."

I thought about the summer vacations with siblings and cousins gathered at the beach. I loved taking long walks along the shore, my bare feet on the wet sand, while I sipped my morning coffee. At night, we'd make a fire on the beach and enjoy the night sky late into the evening. It never occurred to me at the time that these activities could be contemplative practices.

"Next is journaling. This can be a challenge for some, but you like to write, so this may be a natural choice. You've been keeping a personal journal for years, but if you choose, you can go much deeper in your writing. You can make it a safe space for Wholly Kathy to begin expressing herself."

"Can you say more about that?"

"Your journal can act as a protected space where she can explore the areas where her inner and outer worlds are not congruent, that gooey space we talked about. Over time, new areas of interest will emerge out of the goo, as will deep conversations, much like the ones we're having."

This felt true and, once again, it was a natural extension of something I was doing sporadically. While I always kept a notebook of personal thoughts, I never considered this to be a formal journaling practice. It would be fun to explore the idea in more depth.

"The next practice will delight those old warrior instincts of yours. It's the practice of taking positive action. This simply means taking a small, intentional step toward a new way of being. You can think of this as a call and response with your inner knowing. It's a safe way to begin trusting your inner wisdom."

This piqued my interest. The image that came to mind was a lab where I was conducting experiments, trying out different ways of living my life.

"The last practice is holding a question. This is a wonderful way to examine your beliefs, traits, characteristics, roles and social connections to determine if they're still the best choices as your butterfly self emerges. Learning to hold a question can help you determine what will stay in your life and what needs to change."

"So I just ask a question and let it sit?"

"Mmm, that sure stirs up Corporate Kathy, doesn't it? Do you know why?"

"No clue."

"Throughout your career, you were always expected to know the answers or know how to find them quickly if you didn't. Now I'm asking you to just let it be."

"Why?"

"Because it opens you to possibilities that stretch beyond your logical mind into the realm of the heart, which invites innovation, connections and creativity."

"We're getting into woo-woo territory."

"Oh, and walking in the mountains talking to a non-physical entity isn't woo-woo?"

"Good point. Keep going, please."

"Thank you. When it comes to holding a question, just remember this: There's power in the asking, in giving yourself permission to not know. We're going to come back to this theme of permission, but for now, just allow the questions to become bigger and more open-ended. They're invitations to help you get curious and go deep as you design your future."

"Wow, that sounds intense."

"It is, but in a different way. The point is to not rush to the answer. Instead, stay open to the mystery, especially when an answer surfaces that you don't expect. Your job is to note it without filtering or judging anything that comes through."

"Okay, I can give it all a try."

"I have no doubt that you'll commit to trying these practices. It's the undoing that I think will be challenging."

"The undoing? What does that mean?"

"It's another way of saying breaking old habits."

"Such as?"

"Forcing action, overcommitting, being hard on yourself, seeing practice as something to conquer or check off the to-do list, for starters."

"Ouch," I said, recoiling from the direct hit.

"That's the old program we're looking to counter. And if I had to sum up all we've covered today, I suggest three things:

1. Find ways to create physical, mental and emotional space for yourself;

2. Stay open to mystery as you live with your questions; and

3. Be kind to yourself. Watch the self-talk and the judgement.

"If you do those three things, you'll begin to find your way out of the goo and finally give your warrior self some well-deserved rest while practicing your sage qualities."

And then she was gone. I walked back home in silence.

SEVENTEEN

t home, I wrote down her suggestions for finding my way out of the goo before I forgot them:

1. Find ways to create physical, mental and emotional space for myself;

2. Stay open to mystery as I live with my questions; and

3. Be kind to myself, watching the self-talk and judgement.

For the next few days, I felt like I was living two different lives. It was as if I was going about my daily tasks while watching myself from above. It was a different kind of bifurcation. The goo began to feel like quicksand.

I pushed myself to walk the trails, but it was quiet. I longed to hear the word *sweetheart*. Where did she go? I had questions.

Instead, I used those walks to reflect and hold my questions. I became hyperaware of my surroundings and the deepening season. I watched myself focus on the smallest creature crossing my path, then looked up at the vast sky and took in the totality of life in ways I never had before.

I continued to work each day, promoting the book and scouting for business, but I noticed my relief when I woke to a day with no scheduled meetings. On a personal level, I found myself saying no to almost every invitation to connect online and felt good about those decisions. I turned off the news and my phone notifications. I began journaling after my breathing practice in the morning.

The business pressures didn't subside, but underneath it all, there was a depth and a rhythm to my life that surprised me. It was so quiet, yet I felt so connected. But I also felt something stirring, a powerful tremor, emotional plate tectonics, that scared me to acknowledge. It was like some sort of muscular force, which if unleashed, would swallow me whole.

Late one afternoon on the mountain trail, a hidden dam burst. Without warning, tears began to stream.

There was no sorrow or joy, just streams of unrelenting tears. I made my way home hoping not to see any neighbors as I neared my driveway. How would I explain my emotional state? I had no idea what was happening, but it was clear I was falling apart.

It didn't matter what I did. If I read a story, I'd be moved to tears. If I stared out the window, the natural beauty would overtake me. I couldn't bear the thought of speaking to anyone.

I was glad it was Saturday so I'd have the weekend to sort this all out. Just as I thought the tears subsided, they would start again. My eyes reddened and my face got sore from wiping away the cascade of tears.

By the time Sunday arrived, I didn't know what to do with myself. I collapsed in a heap on the couch, recalling a story I once read in *The Sun*. It was about a man who looked down at his chest to find it being plowed by a tiny machine, as if in an open field.

That image was exactly what I was experiencing. It felt like my insides were being broken apart and rearranged after a long winter, like the ground of my unplowed field was being turned and prepared for planting.

I dragged myself off the couch and leafed through a stack of earmarked magazines until I found the article. As I reread the piece, I was reminded that there was a little man driving the tractor, preparing the ground for the Sower, a reference to the biblical parable.

The writer knows it's his life that will be harvested and he was chosen for a reason. In the last image, the driver offers a left-handed salute as he turns the tractor toward its next row. The last three words are, "plows deeper still."

The author used the word *harrowing* in his piece. I walked back to my computer to look up the unfamiliar term. I learned that a harrow is a farming implement that's pulled behind a tractor to break up soil clods and level the surface for planting. It's a process that uses tines or discs.

Discs – there was that word again. I stumbled on it when I was researching metamorphosis and found the term imaginal discs, the dormant cell clusters embedded in caterpillars that were the blueprint for their butterfly selves.

Was I being readied for something? Waves of tears continued.

What I longed for the most was some sage advice. But it was quiet.

I felt like I passed a point of no return. "How am I going to operate in this world?" I asked out loud, pleading to no one.

EIGHTEEN

On Monday morning, I opened my eyes and waited for the barrage of tears. Nothing. A good sign. I was exhausted. And raw to my core. The thought of doing my breathing practice made me shudder.

I got up and moved in slow motion. I stumbled into the shower and let the warmth stream over my aching body, then headed to the kitchen to make coffee. Even though my body felt like it had gone 12 rounds in a title fight, the tears had stopped. As I sipped the inky brew, I decided to take a walk.

I was about 100 yards up the mountain path when I heard, "My, my, sweetheart, look at you."

Hearing that voice was like finally hearing from a long lost friend. It brought me to tears. Here we go again.

"You did an amazing job taking my suggestions to heart, love. You created space for Wholly Kathy and invited mystery as you held your questions. But the self-compassion part, well, we'll have to work on that, won't we?"

She could have recited the alphabet and I wouldn't have cared. I was just so damn happy to have her back.

"Where'd you go?" I asked, trying not to sound as desperate as I felt.

"Well, sweetheart, this was all about connecting with your still point, and I didn't want to interfere. You did know I was close by though, didn't you?"

She sounds so compassionate. I must look like hell.

"Well, you're not looking like your warrior self at the moment, that's for sure."

I was too tired to even laugh. "What's happening to me?"

"Well, sweetheart, the short answer is you're deep in the goo."

"And the long answer?"

"Let's revisit our caterpillar metaphor. The caterpillar does a lot of preparation before entering the cocoon. It expends a lot of energy as it eats and grows as much as it can before spinning the chrysalis. That's what you've done this past year as you got yourself ready to leave your corporate world and create your business.

"After all of that activity, in the quiet of the cocoon, there's only silence and darkness. In this solitude, the caterpillar shrinks, sheds its skin, and dissolves. It resembles nothing of its former self. While it appears to die, the makings of its new self are very much alive. Its cells are waiting for the right time to rearrange into a new structure, transforming the caterpillar into a butterfly.

"In human terms, this is liminal space, where your old identity is dissolving. You're no longer who you were, yet it's unclear who you'll become. In the safety of your cocoon, it can get messy. You can feel unraveled, like you're coming apart at the seams. You can feel out of control at times and unrecognizable, even to yourself."

"Unraveled, yep, that's the word, that's me."

"It's a classic case of identity loss. And it's so, so healthy for you."

"Healthy? I'm a mess. And all I want is to be by myself."

"Yes, love, it's natural to want to withdraw and isolate yourself in these tender times. You're changing dramatically while life around you remains the same. Your loved ones, community, your outer world, they're all going about their usual business, even in these unusual times. It's not uncommon to feel out of place. It can be a confusing time for you and anyone else who knew the old you."

"I don't have the words to even talk to anyone about this, except you. So what's the solution, become a recluse?"

"Oh far from it, sweetheart. Just be patient. The trick is to recognize when it's time to encourage your true identity to slowly emerge from the goo, transforming your old self into your new self. It's up to you to instruct your new DNA, metaphorically speaking."

The walking helped me assimilate all she shared, but something still eluded me. "You mentioned a word before, *liminal*. Tell me more."

"Liminal space is when you're between two stages of life. The word *liminal* means threshold. You're on the threshold of a new way of being, but you're neither in the old space nor the new one.

"It's like standing in a doorway between two rooms where a new life awaits in the room that you're just about to enter. The threshold is an exciting place where you experience identity transformation, but it's also a place of not knowing, which is causing your distress and anxiety."

"It's so strange. I feel paralyzed, yet I'm aware I'm changing in profound ways. The thing is, I know how to operate in the old room. I have no idea what I'll do or what I'll find when I crawl out of the goo and cross the threshold to the new room."

"Ah, but this is all part of it, love. When you cling to the past, the process can be overwhelming and filled with fear, worry and apprehension. When you mindfully help yourself, there's more ease crossing the threshold."

"How do I mindfully help myself?"

"Well, there are two ways to invite ease as you transform. The first is to decide what you'd like to keep in your life and then give yourself permission to let go of whatever is no longer useful. This includes old habits, expectations, relationships, situations, assumptions, and the way you wish things were, to name a few. Think of it as shedding your old skin."

I nodded and she kept going.

"The second is to relax in the goo. You do that by being okay with what's unfolding as you experience the shapeless, formless, embryonic state of what's next."

"The first one sounds easier than the second."

"For you, perhaps. I know it's not easy for you to just be. But that's why you practice. Think of what you've done so far. You've created space in your life so you could practice and you've given yourself permission to change. Now that the old you has started dropping away, you're questioning assumptions."

"What does that mean?"

"Think of it as reviewing Corporate Kathy's standard operating procedures."

"I had SOPs?"

"Well, they weren't formal ones. Remember when I said you had deep grooves and it made you flinch? It's about questioning those unconscious repetitive habits.

"That's what happens naturally as you begin to relax in the goo and let go of what no longer serves. The deeper you go with this, the easier it will be when you begin making life decisions that impact your loved ones, especially in the beginning when they're not prepared and don't know how to support the new you just yet."

It was all so much to absorb. My mind started to spin again.

"The key is self-compassion."

"I know the term, but I don't really know what it means."

"Self-compassion is simply comforting and soothing yourself as you would a friend in need."

"Why is it so important?"

"The more you practice self-compassion, the more you expand your own capacity for emotional well-being, of clarifying what you need and then giving it to yourself. It's actually quite empowering when you learn you have the ability to give yourself all you desire."

I felt my face scrunch up like I had a question with no words. She picked up on it immediately.

"Don't overcomplicate it, sweetheart. You're already doing it."

"I am?"

"Yes, in the mornings when you do your breathing practice, that's self-compassion. You're using soothing touch and giving yourself the gift of quiet space and inner connection."

"Hmm," was all I could muster as I reflected on how I felt when I did that practice first thing in the morning. Now I understood why it made me feel so good.

"Here's how you can take that practice one step further. As you settle into your breathing with your hand over your heart, silently ask yourself, *What do I need most in this moment*?

"Once you get a sense of what would feel good on that morning, give it to yourself. It might be to stay there longer or to go outside to breathe and greet the day. Maybe you need the feeling of safety or comfort.

"If there's nothing in particular, just go on with your day. It's like a friend asking if you need anything. Sometimes you have a need they can fill and other times you just appreciate the asking. Experiment and see what comes up for you.

"And don't forget to journal. You can reflect on self-compassion and also explore ways of letting go and relaxing in the goo. Most of all, sweetheart, remember to keep breathing deeply. You're going to look back on this time with such wonder and fondness someday."

Something about those words felt true, but that outcome seemed so far away. It was clear that our time together had come to an end. I turned around on the trail and headed home.

NINETEEN

For days it felt like the little plow in my chest was working overtime. The more I tried to soothe myself, the deeper it dug. I could feel the metaphorical blades turning the clumps of my soul, bringing up the nutrients to prepare fertile soil for new growth. It hurt like hell.

Even so, I kept up with my daily practices. In the afternoons, when I could muster the strength, I picked up my journal and tried to list what I'd like to keep, what I could release and ways I could relax into my cocoon of goo.

Most days, I came up short and resorted to wandering around the house and doing the mindless administrative tasks that most business owners push aside. I did the accounting, made website updates, and cleared a backlog of emails. It was the only kind of work I felt capable of doing.

My sleep was erratic. Some nights it was filled with fragmented dreams of open doorways on a mountaintop with long, treacherous paths leading to them. Other nights, the imagery was even darker, like a deserted city street where I could sense, but couldn't see, figures just out of my peripheral line of vision. After a few restless nights, I would tumble into a deep sleep for 10 hours and wake in the same position I fell asleep.

Each morning, I would roll onto my back, place my hand over my heart, and breathe, which usually resulted in tears streaming down my face. I was in an endless loop.

After one of those 10 hour deep sleep nights, I felt strong enough for a walk up the mountain. Without summoning her, I heard, "It's good to see you walking, sweetheart. How are you feeling?"

"Gooey," I said. "And exhausted."

"Yes, I see that. Isn't it interesting that the idea of transformation, of becoming a butterfly, is exhilarating, but the progression can be so uncomfortable?" She wasn't looking for a response. "You're feeling a range of emotions because you're being beckoned forward into unknown territory. It's a tiring process to make your own path one step at a time."

"I'll say. What's with the continuous stream of tears?"

"Letting go is grieving, love. Something was lost and it's more than just your career. You locked a lot of emotion away all those years so you could keep your focus on the next achievement. Your tears are a form of unburdening, and, in a sense, relief.

"In addition, you've lost a part of your purpose and identity, along with your daily structure and social connection. Because it's happening in midlife, you're also coming to terms with lost youth and time itself."

Those words landed with unexpected force, like I got the wind knocked out of me. All I could muster was a nod of recognition.

"Believe it or not, sweetheart, you're having an easier time than most because you made the decision to leave and had a plan of what to do next. Think of other people who are unexpectedly asked to leave. When it's unplanned, there's also a loss of control, trust, security and self-confidence. Those folks often wrestle with motivation and clarity on how to move forward."

"So I'm one of the lucky ones," I blurted before I could catch myself.

"I know it may not feel that way, love. It's hard to get your bearings when your inner compass is being recalibrated. But you're doing a great job of acknowledging the poignancy and feeling the heartbreak, which are very real. This is an important step forward.

"You'll move through a number of stages of grief and eventually get to acceptance, which is the beginning of the healing process, of getting stronger, so you can free yourself from the goo. And when things get overwhelming, pause and check-in to remind yourself that in this moment, you're okay."

We walked in silence for quite a while, until I stated the obvious, "I'm so tired of being in the goo."

"Well, sweetheart, the quickest way through is to relax as you feel what you're feeling. When you attach to the familiar, your load will feel heavier and the journey more difficult. The less you resist, the easier the growth process.

"You have a choice. Your natural tendency is to want to control the process, which invites energy that's based in fear and feels constricting. The alternative is to be open to allowing things to unfold in their own time and invite energy based in trust that feels expansive. Both roads will get you there, but the latter approach will help you across the terrain, no matter how difficult, feeling resilient and ready to embrace your life.

"Can you imagine what it would be like to be open to that kind of trust, that whatever life brings your way, you'll have the creativity and resources to respond and thrive? Your willingness to let go will bring you closer to the threshold of your new chapter – one that you get to write."

"That's helpful, thank you," I said.

Her words settled over me, heavy with meaning and light with possibility all at once. I kicked a loose stone along the path, turning the phrase *letting go* in my head over and over.

I realized it was more than just the old professional role – it was the idea of who I had to be to live that life. Yet the notion of letting go and trusting the process felt like the riskiest thing I could ever do.

TWENTY

She broke the long silence with an observation. "You're in some interesting territory, sweetheart. You're in the warmth of the goo, focused on what's been deconstructed. But something is actually beginning to take form. As you've found, it can feel like you're bridging two very different worlds, one that's familiar and one that's elusive, yet compelling.

"Even though you can't see a clear path and you don't have all the answers, it's time to begin taking initial steps toward that intangible vision."

"Okay," I said, suddenly feeling engaged. "What do I do?"

"Ooh, Corporate Kathy is at attention, ready to go!" She nailed me once again.

"Here's the first lesson, love. There are many ways of getting there. Let me try explaining it this way. Picture yourself on a beautiful sailboat. You're in a gorgeous location with endless blue skies and calm seas. The boat is quite large and all the people you love are on the deck, enjoying time together on the water."

I felt myself getting lost in this beach island fantasy.

"But your instinct, sweetheart, is to jump into the water and push the sailboat."

That snapped me out of my reverie. I stopped walking to let that sink in. I could feel my solar plexus catch fire.

She continued, "It's no surprise, is it? You've been wired to move things forward without fail."

I tried to picture myself in the water next to a massive sailboat pushing with all my might.

"What you need to realize is that you have options now. You can hoist the sails and harness wind power. You can start the engine and use mechanical power. You can simply drift, or drop anchor, or dock. But please, love, don't push the sailboat. It'll no longer serve you."

Pow! She landed another punch with ease.

The sting was quickly replaced by realization. "Wow, you're right, that is my instinct!"

I was startled. "How have I not seen this before? I push the sailboat out of habit. For years – no, decades – it was all about pushing by doing my best to make things happen. It felt like inaction to just allow things to unfold. It wasn't even an option!"

"Exactly, very good, sweetheart. Over time, by being mindful, you'll learn to choose *being* rather than *doing*. It's quite the shift."

"Another one of your practices?"

"Actually, sweetheart, it's going to be *your* practice. It's one of becoming. You're becoming your version of the butterfly. It's your way out of the goo."

This got my attention.

"What's next to explore is how you create a life structure that supports the butterfly and not the caterpillar."

"Huh," was all I could muster. "How do I do that?"

"You're in a wonderful place of experimentation. You're slowly learning how to articulate the beginnings of your new life, to embody it for yourself. Over time, you'll get more adept at striking a balance between fully showing up in a new manner and remaining open to the process."

"And not pushing the sailboat?" I couldn't help myself.

"Exactly. As you get used to this dialogue approach with life, you'll feel more in flow with all that can and will be expressed through you."

"We're really getting into woo-woo land now," I joked.

She didn't miss a beat. "Your job is actually quite simple. It's about being aware of how your actions feel as often as possible. Does the next step feel restrictive like a *should,* or does it feel more freeing, like it's a natural, easy progression?

"This is where you'll begin to feel like someone who's more aligned with your new identity and values, where you begin to leave your Type-A urgency and results-oriented drive behind. So when you're on the sailboat deck ready to take the plunge, you can pause and remind yourself there are other ways."

I could hear the playfulness in her voice.

"Does that mean I'm going against my nature?"

"Oh, quite the opposite, sweetheart. You're learning what your true nature is. Let's just say you're learning how to go from Type A to Type Be."

"Type Be, B-E. I like the way that sounds."

"And how does it feel?"

"Like I can breathe."

"Then we're on the right track, sweetheart! This is where you learn to be, to find ways to work hard and take pride in your efforts, but not get stressed. This is where you'll begin to rely on your inner wisdom, on your creative response, and to trust the newfound ease you feel. This is also the place where you'll create more supportive habits for how you want to live. It's all about integrating the elements that make you *you*."

"I suppose you have a practice for me?"

"I do, but it's quite different this time."

This piqued my interest. "Sounds intriguing."

"As intriguing as you'd like it to be. I sense you're up for some adventure, so that's what I'd like you to seek. Be open to a completely new experience."

"That's it? That's my practice?"

"Yes, that's it. And remember to stay on the deck of the sailboat as you glide forward."

TWENTY-ONE

could feel beads of sweat forming on my brow as I looked at my own reflection in a video conference waiting room. I reminded myself to take a few deep breaths. I was safe, sitting in my own kitchen. Why was I so nervous?

At exactly 3:00, my virtual image flickered and I was transported from the waiting room into meeting mode. A fair-skinned, stately woman with gray hair and twinkling blue eyes welcomed me with such wholehearted enthusiasm that I instantly relaxed.

"Hi, I'm Elara!" She beamed, waiting for my introduction.

"I'm Kathy, so nice to meet you."

She looked more like a middle-aged aunt visiting from the Midwest than a mystic healer, sitting in what appeared to be a cabin in the woods. Its furnishings were sparse and neat. A window off to her right side was filled with outdoor greenery. There were bundles of flowers and herbs hanging upside-down from the overhead rafters to dry.

"Nice to meet you," Elara said. "I understand we're connected through Kaitlin?"

"Yes, she's a good friend of mine. She thought a session with you could be…" I searched for the right word… "beneficial."

Elara capably took the reins and began to interview me with the skill of a doctor performing intake procedures in an emergency room, a full scan of my soul to see just what was ailing me. She asked about my physical vitality, my mental and emotional state, my daily stresses and challenges, sleep quality, my work and relationships. I did my best to answer the probing questions succinctly and honestly.

Finally I said, "I'm meeting with you because I'm at a significant crossroads. The way forward seems uncertain and I'm feeling unsettled." It was the understatement of the year.

She leaned down to pick up a hand drum, closed her eyes and began to deftly strike it. I was surprised at how the sound reverberated through my computer speakers, pulsing in my chest and bones. It was oddly hypnotic.

After a few minutes, the drumming slowed and she took a thorough look at me. "Have you ever drummed?"

I shook my head.

The diagnosis continued. "One with your personality type needs to find methods to get out of her own way. Drumming keeps your left brain occupied while you engage with your right brain. I have a feeling this might serve you," she said as she winked.

Then we got down to business. "Close your eyes," she instructed. "Go deep and give me a word or two to describe why you're *really* here."

I closed my eyes and was surprised by my own response that toppled out without warning. "Breaking silence."

I wasn't sure where that phrase came from or what it meant, but she clasped her hands and bounced in her chair as if it brought her great joy, like we were really getting somewhere.

"Okay, then. Why don't you move to a comfortable spot where you can lie down with your eyes closed."

I took the laptop over to the couch and settled in. She suggested I cover myself with a blanket and lightly cover my eyes as well.

She put on some drumming music and told me to visualize myself at a threshold. "Bring to mind an offering you can make for the life experience that brought you to this point."

I was at a loss, unsure what that meant or what to do. She must have sensed my confusion and reassured me. "Just surrender and open to the process. Allow yourself to be absorbed in the swirl of the drumbeats." I began taking deep breaths and focused on each drumbeat that resonated in my body. Then I heard a rattle as her voice weaved in and out, singing unfamiliar words. I lost all track of time.

At some point, there was a sensation that felt like wind moving from the top of my head to my heart. Then the music stopped.

Her gentle voice instructed me to continue to breathe deeply. And whenever I felt ready, to uncover my eyes and sit up.

I opened and closed my hands a few times to get the blood flowing. My arms felt numb as I raised them to remove the covering from my eyes. I felt my face wet with tears.

It took a while to refocus. Then I slowly sat up, feeling altered, but not sure what had shifted.

Elara suggested I close my eyes and just feel my body. I felt tired, bordering on achy, but calm.

We sat in silence for a long while. Then she shared what she experienced on my behalf.

Elara's journey began with a meandering walk through a forest. The healer came upon a tent where a 16-year-old girl was camping all alone as the sun rose.

The young girl was at home in these woods, but was startled the previous night when she heard rustling outside her tent. Alert, she waited and listened before concluding that a pack of wolves was in the area.

As night fell, the wolves began to sing and howl. At first, she was frightened, but decided to join in their song and howled with them for most of the night until she finally slept.

When she woke, she wasn't sure if it was a dream or something she actually experienced. When she unzipped her tent, however, she saw paw prints all around her campsite.

She walked to the stream and bent down to fill her cupped hand with water. In the reflection, she saw a wolf image just over her shoulder. In honor, she lowered her head to the water to drink, as would a wolf.

The healer walked up to the young girl. "Hello, little wolf pup. Some night, huh?"

"You have no idea."

"Pup, would you like to come back?" the healer asked. "Kathy's all grown up now and is about to embark on a big adventure." Pup readily agreed.

Elara summed up her visioning experience by explaining, "That's what felt like wind. You are whole now."

She put on a soundtrack of running water and suggested I close my eyes again. Elara instructed me to visualize a stream, gently submerge myself in it, and let go of anything I no longer needed.

When I opened my eyes, I felt lighter. There was some lingering fatigue, like I physically took a lengthy journey. Elara recommended a quiet afternoon, drinking lots of water, taking a short walk and getting to bed early.

I thanked her for her time. I wasn't sure what she had done or what was healed. I also had no idea what to make of the story of my 16-year-old pup-self. Clearly, there was a lot to process.

TWENTY-TWO

was too tired for a walk. So I filled a big container with water that I sipped as I sat outside, closing my eyes and feeling the setting sun's warmth on my skin. After a light snack, I headed to bed.

When I woke ten hours later, I had questions. I quickly dressed, put on my hiking boots and headed for the path.

It wasn't long before I heard, "Congratulations, sweetheart. Not only did you invite a new adventure, but you stayed on the sailboat the whole time!"

"What was that? A shift in consciousness? A waking dream?"

"Yes," she answered.

"Yes? More please. A sixteen-year-old me hanging out with wolves?"

"Fascinating, isn't it? And all of that insight from an intentional meditation to help you transcend your ordinary routine. Amazing what happens when you let go of what you think you know and open to all the other realms that you can explore, all available to unlock the healing needed in this physical reality."

"Intentional meditation, that's all it was? What about the girl?"

"What about her? That's a question for you to walk with. What drove your 16-year-old self out to the woods for safety? More importantly, how do you welcome her back? Oh, and the wolf, there's significance there as well."

It was all too much. I found a big flat rock near the stream and plopped down. I closed my eyes and just listened to my surroundings.

I'm not sure how long I was there, lost in the sound of the running water.

After a while I heard, "Can you feel the difference?"

I opened my eyes as she continued. "In the past, you would have buried this experience, pushed it out of your mind, if you even allowed yourself to have it. And now, you're sitting with it. Connecting with nature and the calm and ease that's always available to you. Allowing it all to be. Even in your confusion, you're open to its teaching."

"That's true," I said, taking a deep breath. "It still feels confusing – drum, girl, wolves."

"Just stay open to the teaching, sweetheart. You'll get a deeper understanding. And don't be surprised if it's quite simple. That's usually how it works."

And with that, I knew I was back on my own.

TWENTY-THREE

As I went about my days, I could feel summer was coming to a close. The skies darkened earlier each evening and there was a slight chill in the air most mornings. My routine hadn't altered all that much – the gym, my work, and the walks – but something shifted inside energetically. I couldn't quite put my finger on what exactly had changed, but clearly something had.

It was like I was living a koan, an unanswerable Zen paradox that defied logic. I knew that was the point. *I can't think my way out of this.* I laughed out loud at the absurdity of that, well, thought.

The sage was right. I'm still on the sailboat and feel no urge to jump in and push it. What does it all mean? I have no idea. Even so, it feels like progress.

Realizing that I wasn't meant to solve the koan, I refocused on my life. From the perspective of my family, friends and colleagues, I was the same person. In fact, they were so wrapped up in their pandemic turmoil that I was given the gift of social cover, working through all of this undetected.

The questions that seemed most relevant had less to do with the wolf and more to do with the butterfly. I could feel my wings starting to form. The cocoon was getting restrictive. I knew I would be breaking out of it soon. And what would that mean for me? For my work? For my life?

It was the perfect morning to take a walk. The temperature was in the mid-70s and the sun darted in and out of huge cumulus cloud formations. I was energized by the day and an unfamiliar sense of buoyancy that felt nourishing.

As I walked up the hill, I did something strange. My right hand instinctively tapped my thigh twice and I silently summoned the wolf. In my mind's eye, a gorgeous husky-looking canine sauntered alongside me.

I was so taken by its beauty, I didn't even question if this was my imagination. It was mostly gray and black, about 5 feet long and 125 pounds with a large bushy tail. It was graceful and methodical as it made its way up the mountain.

We were almost to the top of the trail when I heard, "Well, sweetheart, I see you brought a friend today."

"So, this isn't my imagination?"

"It's as fantastical as you make it. I like to call it inspiration. After all, it's coming from a place deep inside of you."

Her words lingered as I took a deep breath of mountain air. I looked at the wolf again. It was magnificent, moving with such agility and its piercing eyes seemed to miss nothing. Given his size, I surmised he was male.

"He's…incredibly aware," I said, "constantly scanning the periphery, alert to every rustle, every shift in the breeze."

"That's true," she said. "Wolves have highly developed senses, making them hyper-alert to their environment and potential threats. That's how they survive as predators in the wild, by constantly evaluating the landscape for variables and being ready to act at all times."

I nodded. Her words brought a familiar tension that continued building between my shoulder blades. I gently moved my neck to ease the tightness, but it brought little relief.

"Hyper-alert. That's how I used to feel – all the time. It was my job to anticipate every possible risk, every failure point. Back then, my biggest fear was to miss something, to be blindsided by an event we should have caught. It never happened, but the ongoing pressure meant I was in a constant state of readiness.

"The corporate term for it was *situational awareness*. We continuously observed and gathered information, noted patterns and trends that led to threats, and then recommended proactive planning. Sounds benign now, but it included operational disruptions, security breaches and the impact from an everchanging business landscape."

The sage listened and then spoke. "And now, sweetheart, you've stepped away from that corporate landscape. You're building something new, something aligned with your heart. Yet, could it be that the same constant state of readiness is still operating within you, even without the external threats that once demanded it?"

"Yeah, it's like I'm staying on the sailboat now, but I've got the engine at full throttle. And that's not the point of having a sailboat, is it?"

"No, love, it's not. But consider this. What if that is precisely why the wolf has chosen to appear to you now? What if those very qualities – the hyper-alertness, the relentless vigilance, the perpetual readiness – are what he's here to carry for you?"

"Carry for me? How?"

"Imagine it," she said, "everything you described: being on guard, micro-managing the unknown, the pressure to control every possible outcome. Gather it. See the dense energy that resides within you."

I paused on the trail so I could close my eyes and was surprised that a visual came quickly. I imagined a grey swirl of energy in my solar plexus, its arms circulating like a hurricane.

She continued her instruction. "Now, with each exhaled breath, offer that energy to the wolf. Visualize it flowing from your body to his form. He's strong enough to hold it. It's his nature to be watchful, so you no longer need to be."

I did as she suggested, taking a deep breath and pushing the energy in his direction as I exhaled. I continued this for a few breaths, taking air in and consciously directing that energy toward the wolf. I felt him standing still, staring straight ahead, accepting his new assignment. With each exhale, I felt more and more of a release.

"Nice work, sweetheart," she said. "How do you feel?"

I opened my eyes and did a quick body scan. Words came out of my mouth that I never heard myself utter before. "I feel… protected."

TWENTY-FOUR

We walked in silence for a long time before I asked the obvious question. "Am I breaking out of the cocoon?"

"I think you know the answer to that question, sweetheart."

"Am I ready?"

"It's up to you to be ready. And I'm here to help. You've done the hard work of creating a new identity. But there are practical questions to consider.

"How do you build an environment that supports the butterfly and allows her to take flight? What type of life do you really want to live? How do you become someone capable of living that life?

"Remember what summoned me. You did a future self meditation that brought me into your realm. It might be a good time to have another shape-shifting experience."

Those words resonated deep in my soul. I could feel my eyes moisten, what I came to recognize as a sign of truth.

"I think it's time for you to experiment with your developing wings a bit, to test them out. Let's take a little leap, your first flight. It's only through action that you can explore how something feels."

"Yeah, that feels right," I said. "What do you have in mind?"

"Tonight, we'll experience our first night walk."

"What?!" I stopped in my tracks, stomach seizing, solar plexus ablaze as the sound of my voice echoed in the empty woods. "I've never been on these trails at night!"

She was very matter-of-fact and instructional. "I suggest packing things that will keep you nourished and warm. Some tobacco and sage would be a nice touch. Oh, and don't forget fire starting materials."

"What? Wait, I'm not ready for this!"

"Time to fly, sweetheart. Trust that you'll know what to do. I'll see you when the sun sets at the old Girl Scout camp."

TWENTY-FIVE

spent the afternoon muttering to myself, mostly versions of "How did I get myself into this?" Rummaging in the basement, I found a tent, sleeping bag and backpack, used only once when I attended an outdoor festival with friends years ago.

There was a headlamp in the backpack, but the batteries leaked from lack of use. I cleared as much caked acid from the compartment as I could and popped in new batteries. To my surprise, it worked.

I gathered a few fatwood fire starter sticks and a lighter from the container near the fireplace, along with some bug repellent and bear spray from the mudroom and a small hatchet from the garage. I tossed an apple, some trail mix, a liter of water and a few protein bars in the bag, along with some rolled up toilet paper, hand wipes and a few plastic bags.

As the afternoon wore on, I racked my brain. What else? She suggested bringing tobacco and sage, neither of which I had. I jumped in the car and headed to the grocery store, picking up a pouch of American Spirit loose rolling tobacco and a bottle of sage leaves from the spice section. It would have to do.

Even with all the busyness, I questioned my sanity. I was about to head into the woods by myself at night because a disembodied voice made the suggestion. I was either breaking out of my cocoon or losing my mind.

A nervous nausea took hold as the sky darkened. I glanced over at my gear, propped up by the door. There was still time to back out.

I closed my eyes, put my hand over my heart and took a deep breath. What was I really afraid of?

A lot of animals roamed these mountains, including bears and coyotes. A neighbor recently told me he'd seen a mountain lion. I had also seen evidence of make-shift shelters deep in the woods, so a drifter was also a possibility.

Maybe the biggest fear was that if something happened, no one would know where I was. But I decided not to tell anyone where I was headed. How could I explain it? A voice told me to meet her at an abandoned scout camp at night?

So I left a note on my whereabouts, just in case. It was simple: "Went camping at Girl Scout Camp." As I wrote it, I thought, *at least they'll know where to find the body.*

I continued with my breathing practice as night fell. To my surprise, my stomach calmed considerably. In fact, my whole body eased and I was present and focused. I was ready.

The pack was heavy, filled with gear I wasn't even sure I needed. My quads strained as the path steepened, my breath labored from the load. As I had done earlier in the day, my right hand tapped my thigh twice to summon the wolf. Almost instantly, the faithful canine walked beside me, then took the lead, a protective move that comforted me.

The scout camp was about a mile and a half up the path, across a brook and tucked into the belly of the mountain. It would take about a half hour to hike there. I had walked this path countless times during the day, but hiking at night was different.

My senses were heightened to the point of overload. The moon was almost full, which provided more than enough light for my adjusted eyes to navigate the path, no headlamp needed. I was aware of the slightest movement, like the breeze murmuring through the tree canopy gently rustling the leaves, and the water in the stream gurgling downhill over the rocks. There was the occasional sound of a small animal finding its way through the dry grasses mingled with the crunch of my own footsteps. With each strained breath, I inhaled the complex earthy scent of it all.

I was so lost in thought that she startled me. "I'm so proud of you, sweetheart. I wasn't sure you'd show, but look at you, outfitted just like a pro. You're a natural!"

I smiled and kept walking. Hearing her voice and seeing the silhouette of the wolf ahead added to my tranquil state.

"Let's make the most of this walk, shall we? How are you feeling about this adventure?"

I checked in with myself. "Well, the terror I felt as I was preparing for this excursion has subsided. I feel some excitement, a lot of curiosity…and there's something different stirring, but I can't name it."

"That's simply your heart opening to the experience. It's a good sign. It's the expansion needed to break free of the cocoon."

I let her words seep in.

"Can you tell me a little about this evening?" I asked as I shifted my pack to ease the deep ridges that were indented in my shoulders from the weight.

"I'd sum it up like this. You've been asking a lot of questions these past few months. Tonight, you'll be entering the space for answers."

We walked in silence for a while and then she spoke. "Since this is new to you, I'll share a few thoughts, but keep in mind that the whole purpose of this evening is for you to go by your instinct.

"I suggest you use the bridge that leads into the camp as your threshold, a way to leave the old behind and cross into the new. Once you cross over, you'll be on your own. Do what feels right. Make an offering to the land, find a way to ready yourself and the space, and be open to the unfolding. Most importantly, listen."

"That's helpful, thank you," I said, as I noticed the wolf turned and stopped. We were at the bridge. Once I crossed the stream, I'd be on my own.

"One more thing, sweetheart. What is the question you most want answered?"

The reply immediately came to mind. "When I had that healing session with Elara, she asked why I really came to see her. Without warning, I said, 'Breaking silence.' I still have no idea why I said that.

"And then, at the end of our session, she told me about my 16-year-old self that went into the woods to live amongst the wolves. I'd like to know what it all means. For some reason it feels relevant."

"Those are wonderful questions to hold."

"So, this is it? It's time?"

"It's time, sweetheart. Have faith. You'll know exactly what to do."

TWENTY-SIX

turned to my left to face the bridge. I paused and took a few deep breaths before walking across, the wolf by my side. Each step was intentional as I mindfully left the old behind and welcomed the new. I was on my own.

On the other side of the bridge, there was a long path leading up to the camp. I methodically wound my way up the hill until I came to a clearing. In the distance, I could make out the silhouette of old camping cabins, thanks to the light of the moon. They were arranged in a semi-circle in various stages of disrepair.

In the middle of the clearing, there were remnants of a stone fire ring, surrounded with rocks that once served as seats from a long ago jamboree. I dropped my pack and got to work.

First, I made the fire ring serviceable by rearranging the rocks and adding new ones from the surrounding grounds. I grabbed the hatchet and ventured to the edge of the forest to collect kindling and wood, taking an armload at a time to the fire pit.

Once the wood was gathered, I moved a few of the smaller boulders together and unrolled my sleeping bag to make a comfortable seat. Then I placed some kindling and fatwood in the fire pit and arranged the logs in a pyramid shape around the twigs.

While I went about my tasks, I replayed the sage's instructions in my head. *Find a way to ready yourself and the space, make an offering to the land, do what feels right, be open to the unfolding, listen…*

I found my way down to the stream to wash my hands and splash water on my face. The water was cold and stimulating. Out of the corner of my eye, I saw the wolf wandering near the water's edge.

I flashed back to my session with Elara, the healer, who told the story of my 16-year-old self hidden in the woods amongst the wolves. I peered at my moonlit reflection in water. Instantly, I knew what to do next.

I made my way back to the fire ring and lit the kindling. It took some coaxing, but the wood eventually caught. I reached into my bag for the tobacco, holding the pouch to my heart as I looked up to the sky.

"Thank you for this opportunity…" was all I could think to say because I wasn't sure what the night would bring. I sprinkled tobacco as I walked around the outside of the circle, asking for protection and insight as to why my younger self felt the need to retreat to the woods and what silence needed to be broken.

I stowed the tobacco in my pack and retrieved the sage leaves. I emptied the bottle in my hand and threw the contents in the fire.

The fire billowed and I took a deep breath of its sweet earthy scent. Reaching into its plume with cupped hands, I guided the smoke toward me, letting it settle over my head and body. I felt cleansed.

I threw more logs on the fire, which made it spark and pop. Then I walked back to my sleeping bag and settled in on the rocks I'd arranged for myself.

As the fire blazed, I noticed the tree frogs began their chorus. As the sound level amplified, it reminded me of a high pitched version of Elara's drumming.

I sat cross-legged with one of the rocks supporting my lower back and relaxed. As I closed my eyes, I could feel the rhythmic sound pulsing throughout my body. The more I focused, the more it intensified. I'm not sure how long I sat there, but when I opened my eyes, I was not alone.

TWENTY-SEVEN

was startled but didn't dare move, aside from my eyes, which darted from figure to figure. My heart pounded as I tried to determine who had joined my circle. I blinked to bring the scene into focus.

Sitting crossed-legged in front of me, across the fire, was a teenage girl, with eyes that appeared back-lit. To my left was a buttoned-up woman, her intense stillness charged with unwavering vigilance. To my right was another woman, her smile warm and presence emanating deep serenity. When I turned my head to the left, I saw the wolf sitting beside me, staring straight ahead. To my immediate right was a white haired woman, also quietly looking into the fire.

I remembered what the sage told me on the walk up. "You've been asking a lot of questions these past few months. Tonight, you'll be entering the space for answers." I continued to sit quietly and gaze into the flames.

I couldn't tell if it was the fire or the moonlight making mischief, but their forms seemed to shimmer, as if they were dressed in flowing luminescent garments. The girl spoke first.

"I'm Pup, and I've waited a long time for this conversation. I'm glad you chose to make this journey." She paused, gathering her thoughts.

"Think back to your teenage years. You knew you wanted to live a non-traditional, independent life, yet there were long established family and societal expectations you needed to manage. Even at that young age, you knew there would be compromises and hard choices.

"That's why you sent me here. I kept your essence, the wildness of your soul, intact while you quietly walked your path, conforming to the extent you needed to achieve the success you wanted. It was an act of self-preservation, a natural instinct, so you could make your necessary personal and professional choices."

Before I could even process how mind-blowing it was to sit across from my younger self, the buttoned-up woman to my left spoke.

"Once you disengaged from your younger self, you focused all that energy into me, Corporate Kathy, striving for higher and higher standards. We were on that corporate treadmill together for decades, always reaching for the next rung of the ladder. It was your way of feeling in control."

All I could do was nod my head in agreement. Then the smiling woman to my right spoke and when she did, I recognized her as Elara.

"That's why Wall Street was the perfect place for you in those early years. Bright lights in the big city where the party never ended to keep you absorbed, numb and self-medicated."

I flashed back to my younger years and winced at a hazy tumble of memories, marveling that I made it through as unscathed as I did.

Elara continued. "All the activity and the substances were like Novocain, distancing you from the void you felt inside."

Pup added, "The sporadic flicker of aliveness you felt in quiet moments at the beach or staring at the night sky, that was me, reminding you I was here and inviting you back."

I knew exactly what she was talking about. The times I drove cross-country, far from New York City, making my way through the national parks or enjoying beach vacations. Yeah, I remembered those sparks and how calm I was in their wake.

Pup gave me time to reflect before she concluded. "The times when you almost worked yourself to emotional and physical exhaustion could have been catastrophic. But they weren't, because I held your identity. And I was always there beckoning you to envision a new way forward."

Another flash of recognition struck as I remembered the time, on the brink of burnout, when a Pup-sent spark in the Alaskan wilderness crystalized the end of my Wall Street career and the beginning of a fundamentally different path.

No one spoke for a long while, as I gazed at the night sky. Up to this point, I hadn't uttered a word. But I had a burning question I needed to ask.

I turned to Elara. "What does *breaking silence* mean?"

She stared into the fire for a long time before answering. "This is a deep generational pattern. You shrouded your true self to avoid the risk of rejection and judgment. Your safety and shelter was silence. It represents all the ways you've denied yourself. Any time you didn't trust your instincts or second-guessed yourself. Whenever you suppressed your feelings and avoided your emotions. The times you were not in alignment with your beliefs and values. In other words, all the times you pleased others or hid your heart."

Each sentence fragment hit like shrapnel.

"Now you see you have the desire and the power to break that silence by living out loud, in whatever damn way you please."

I smiled, hadn't seen that coming.

Elara had more to offer. "The gift of this time together is to show you just how far you've come. You've reimagined your path and opened to alternative ways that align with your beliefs and values. You're no longer concerned with anyone else's expectations or agenda. You trust in your abilities and come from a place of love and compassion for yourself and others. As you surround yourself with people who understand and support your true self, you'll guide and encourage others. You have so much to share. And to celebrate."

Elara placed her hands together as if in prayer and bowed. I returned the gesture.

Corporate Kathy spoke next. "Congratulations on your metamorphosis. You're ascending a new ladder of your choosing. This one is more like a beautiful staircase to your envisioned future. I applaud your effort to journey from your head to your heart, from your Type A self to your Type Be self. Rest assured, I'll still be here to balance and support you along the way." We nodded to each other in appreciation.

It was Pup's turn to speak. "Elara already returned your essence, your wildness, during your healing session. Make room for it to flourish. Let go of what no longer serves you. Mindfully reconnect with anything you suppressed, denied or ignored. When life feels beautiful and expansive, you'll know you're on the right track. I'll always be here, too, anytime you want to play in nature."

In lieu of a bow, the girl extended her arm in a fist bump gesture. I laughed and raised my arm to align with hers across the fire.

Finally, the sage spoke. I turned my body to the right to face her. "This is the heroine's journey. It culminated when you stepped over the bridge to the new and welcomed all parts of yourself back. All of your experiences were important to create who you are today. This ceremony has been a way to honor and integrate all the parts of who you are – what a beautiful gift.

"I suggest you rest now. When you feel ready to cross back over the threshold, you have the opportunity to complete the journey by sharing that gift with your community. The wolf will always be there to protect you. And you can call on us anytime for support as you live out your true life purpose: To create wholeness and connection through story.

"Welcome home, sweetheart."

I placed my hand over my heart as we bowed to each other.

Taking the sage's advice, I reclined and pulled my sleeping bag around me, staring at the glowing embers of the fire.

I reflected on what she described as my true life purpose to create wholeness and connection through story. As I focused on those words, I could feel my fully formed wings expand and knew it was time to fly.

EPILOGUE

Long shadows stretched across the dramatic slopes of Big Sur. The Pacific Ocean glistened in the distance and the scent of salt and eucalyptus drifted on the breeze that rustled the towering redwoods surrounding the pristine retreat center.

A deep, centering breath flowed into me, effortless now, filling my lungs with wild, vibrant air. I felt the earth's grounding energy rise through my hiking boots, rooting me where I stood.

It was a visceral contrast to the rapid breathing and tense muscles that once shouldered the invisible weight of my former life. This wasn't just my work, it was my very being, in true harmony.

I looked out at the accomplished group gathered before me, dressed in the casual comfort of retreat wear. Their faces, though weary and in need of a much deserved break, held a quiet anticipation for what was ahead. They had made a sizeable investment in themselves, each seeking deep, personal insight.

"Welcome to a different kind of personal exploration," I began, my voice resonating with a genuine warmth that still took me by surprise. "It's a privilege to spend this time with you in this beautiful space.

"Not so long ago, I was sitting exactly where many of you are now – driven, successful, and perhaps quietly yearning for some deeper meaning. My own journey, which began with gentle steps of growth, was ignited by a profound experience that ultimately helped me embody the simple, yet powerful Sage Walk process we're going to share.

"A Sage Walk isn't just a hike, it's an opportunity to connect with a deeper source of wisdom – the wisdom that already resides, often untapped, within each of you. As you'll soon experience, nature can act as a catalyst, nudging your inner guidance to become readily accessible by inviting you to open your senses fully to the natural world and allow yourself to simply *be*.

"This is a practice I guide my clients through in virtual sessions, though there's nothing quite like experiencing it together, out on the trails, as we will tomorrow. Something magical happens when we share and integrate our learnings together.

"I think you'll be amazed at how this process can help you become not just more personally fulfilled, but, as a natural consequence, better partners, colleagues and leaders. It can shape your personal and professional lives in ways you can't imagine right now.

"My role here is to be a guide, to offer some tools, and most importantly, create a sacred space for you to connect with yourselves in a new way. This is a safe space to let go of the familiar, to embrace the unknown, and to discover the profound insights that emerge when you slow down, observe and listen.

"Perhaps some of you aren't ready for a complete life overhaul – and that's perfectly okay. It took me years to turn my corporate experience, which I'm very proud of, into an entrepreneurial adventure. So we'll start gently and meet you where you are.

"The Sage Walk process will help you hear your own guidance so you can identify the necessary pivot point, gain clarity on what's essential for you at this time in your life, and begin moving in a direction that feels more aligned, genuine and sustainable.

"The good news is, you won't leave here with anything added to your to-do list. You'll leave with something far more valuable: a powerful, actionable reframe that will change how you see and approach everything you do.

"Over dinner, I'll share more about how this intentional practice transformed my life, along with stories of others who found renewed purpose and built lives that resonated for them.

"Tomorrow morning, we'll set our intentions and then hit the trails to give it a try."

I paused and smiled, feeling the curiosity and sense of adventure building in the room.

"Who's ready for dinner?"

As the group began to gather their belongings and head toward the lodge, I heard that familiar voice.

"You go, sweetheart!"

Thank you for walking with the sage.

In addition to her books, Kathy has numerous resources she makes available for readers of *Walking with the Sage*.

They are available at:
https://athenawellness.com/sagebook

ABOUT THE AUTHOR

KATHY ROBINSON was 25 years into a successful corporate career, and the Chief Audit Executive and Chief Risk Officer of a Fortune 250 company, when she began to feel a quiet yearning for a different kind of fulfillment.

This personal transition—from corporate professional to the founder of Athena Wellness—is the inspiration behind her work. In *Walking with the Sage*, she uses a compelling modern parable to illustrate the very transition she experienced: moving from a mindset of relentless doing to a space of mindful being, from Type A to Type Be.

Now drawing on her expertise as a certified wellness coach, Kathy supports leaders and entrepreneurs who are experiencing midlife transitions and feel the pull toward something more. Through her experiential coaching, facilitated workshops and nature-based retreats, her unique approach bridges business acumen with a holistic coaching methodology, guiding clients to access their inner wisdom and use the natural world as a catalyst for insight.

A CrossFit enthusiast, dedicated hiker and Sierra Club outings leader, Kathy lives the principles she teaches and believes the greatest investment we can make is in our own well-being – a return that yields vitality, engagement and purpose.

To learn more about Kathy, visit https://athenawellness.com.

To contact Kathy for coaching, facilitating or speaking opportunities, email hello@athenawellness.com.

You can also connect with Kathy at:
LinkedIn: https://linkedin.com/in/ kathybrobinson-athenawellness/

www.ingramcontent.com/pod-product-compliance
Lightning Source LLC
Chambersburg PA
CBHW071441130726
47997CB00006B/2180